Super Explorers

SPACE

Tamara Hartson

What is Space?

Space is also sometimes called outer space. It is the dark and starry place beyond Earth. The planet Earth is in space, just like the Sun and the Moon.

Even though space looks like it is full of stars, it is really quite empty. The distance between stars in space is very far.

Many interesting things are found in space, such as planets, stars, galaxies, nebulas, asteroids and comets.

Our solar system has 8 planets that circle around the Sun. Some planets have moons. Earth has one moon, and Jupiter has 67!

The eight planets showing their size differences and arranged in order: Mercury, Venus, Earth, Mars, Jupiter, Saturn, Uranus and Neptune.

Sun

The Sun is the center of the solar system. It is also called Sol. The Sun produces light, heat and energy. Without the Sun, life could not survive on Earth.

Earth

Our Home

Earth is the fifth largest planet in the solar system. Most of Earth is covered by oceans. More than 8 million kinds of life live on Earth, including about 7 billion humans.

The Aurora Borealis is also known as Northern Lights. Auroras are caused by particles from the Sun mixing with Earth's magnetic field. Winter is the best time to see an aurora.

Aurora Borealis

Sometimes an aurora is red. Auroras are red when they are high above the earth.

Auroras are common around the north and south poles. An aurora at the south pole is called Aurora Australis. When seen from space, an aurora looks like a curtain of shimmering light.

Planets sometimes have moons. Earth has only one moon, called Luna. Our moon is large and easy to see from Earth. The rise and fall of ocean tides on Earth are caused by the gravity of our moon.

Moon

The Sun shines on the Moon. As the Moon revolves around Earth, we see different parts of the sunlit moon. These are known as the phases of the moon. The Moon changes from a thin crescent to a full moon and back again every month.

Moon Phases

This phase of the moon is called a half moon.

First Quarter
Half Moon

Waxing
Crescent

Waxing
Gibbous
Moon

New Moon
(Moon is not
visible)

Full Moon

Here are all the phases of the moon.

Waning
Crescent

Waning
Gibbous
Moon

Three Quarter
Half Moon

Man on the Moon

Humans cannot live on the Moon because there is no air. Astronauts have to wear special space suits with air tanks so they can breathe.

People have made 9 trips to the Moon. Each trip was called an Apollo Mission. In total, 12 astronauts have walked on the Moon. The Moon has less gravity than Earth, so walking on the Moon is like bouncing very slowly. You could easily jump as high as a 6-storey buiding!

The **Lunar Roving Vehicle** is a special type of car that astronauts took to the Moon. Three different cars were made and taken to the Moon. All three are still there!

This footprint on the surface of the Moon was made by astronaut Buzz Aldrin, and it will stay there for a long, long time because there is no wind or water to move the dust.

Mercury is the smallest planet and the closest to the sun. It does not have any moons.

Venus is the most similar to Earth in size, but it is much, much hotter and has acid in its atmosphere!

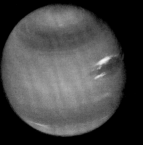

Neptune is the planet farthest from the sun. It is an ice giant. It is large and made of gases and some ice.

Other Planets

Mars has two moons, Phobos and Deimos.

Mars is the fourth planet in the solar system. Mars is a rocky planet. It is very different from Earth because it is smaller and doesn't have oceans. The air on Mars is thin and has little oxygen.

Mars

The planet Mars has polar ice caps just like Earth.

The surface of Mars looks like a rocky desert. The rocks have lots of iron, so the planet looks red. People often call Mars the Red Planet.

People have never been to Mars. Scientists are planning to build special spacecraft that one day may take astronauts to Mars.

Scientists have sent 4 rovers to Mars. Two of them are still sending information and photos back to us.

Rovers are like small cars that have computers and cameras. Before rovers are sent to Mars, they are built and tested here on Earth at special space research centres.

Mars Missions

The Sun is the closest star to Earth. Light from the Sun takes 8 minutes and 20 seconds to reach Earth. The next closest star to Earth is called Proxima Centauri. Light from this star takes more than 4 years to reach Earth!

Stars

A star is a hot sphere of glowing gas. Stars produce heat, light and energy. We see stars only at night because the light of the Sun prevents us from seeing them during the day.

The smallest and dimmest stars are tiny red dwarfs. We have found a red dwarf star that is only a bit bigger than Jupiter.

Red Dwarfs & Supergiants

Supernova

When a supergiant star is at the end of its life, it explodes. The explosion is called a supernova. This purple cloud is left over from a massive supernova.

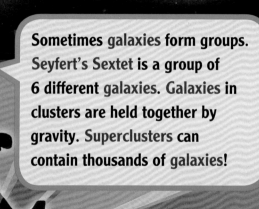

Sometimes galaxies form groups. Seyfert's Sextet is a group of 6 different galaxies. Galaxies in clusters are held together by gravity. Superclusters can contain thousands of galaxies!

Galaxies & Star Clusters

Hoag's Object
Ring Galaxy

More
Galaxies &
Star Clusters

M82 Starburst Galaxy

Pinwheel Galaxy

Christmas Tree Star Cluster

Andromeda Spiral Galaxy

This constellation is often called the Big Dipper because it looks like a scoop.

Since ancient times, people have looked into the night sky and seen shapes in the stars. These shapes are called constellations. Many constellations look like animals, gods and heroes.

Constellations

This is Galaxy M81. It is a spiral galaxy that scientists believe is similar to the Milky Way.

The Milky Way

Our solar system is in a galaxy called the Milky Way. On a clear night far away from any city lights, you can see a thick band of stars. This is the Milky Way.

Black Holes

A black hole is a part of space with very strong gravity. The pull of gravity in a black hole is so powerful, all light and matter disappear into it.

Astronomers today use special computers and telescopes to learn about space.

People used to think Earth was the center of the universe. Nicolaus Copernicus was one of the first astronomers to say that Earth revolves around the Sun.

A long time ago, Galileo Galilei used his telescope to see the movement of the planets. He also discovered the 4 largest moons of Jupiter.

Astronomers

Hubble Telescope

The Hubble Telescope is a special telescope because it was made to work in space. It has been in orbit around Earth for more than 26 years. It takes photos of planets, stars, galaxies and nebulas.

An **astronaut is** trained to fly and work in space and a spacecraft. Most astronauts who go into space stay in orbit around Earth.

Astronaut Neil Armstrong **was** the first person to walk on the Moon. He stepped onto the Moon on July 21, 1969.

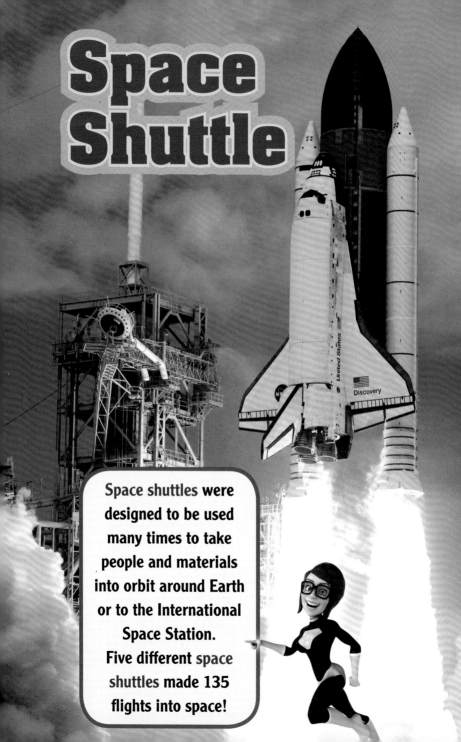

Space Shuttle

Space shuttles **were** designed to be used many times to take people and materials into orbit around Earth or to the International Space Station. Five different space shuttles made 135 flights into space!

Because the **shuttle** is a glider, it had to be carried to the launch site on the back of a plane!

When in orbit, the doors on the back of the **shuttle** open to release equipment and cool the **shuttle**.

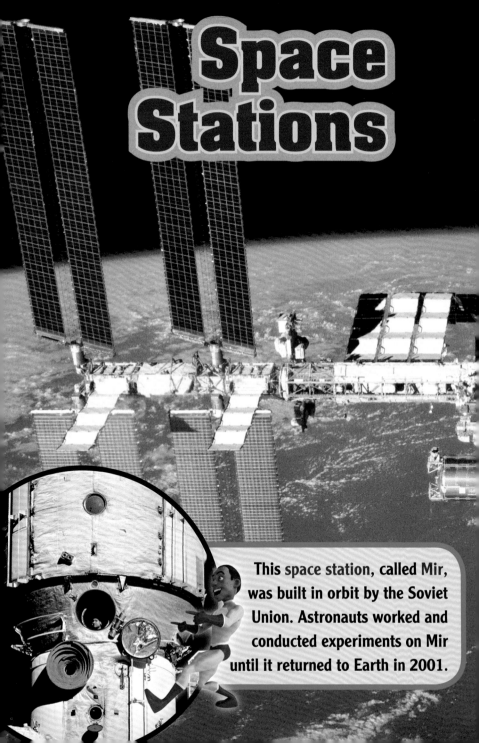

Space Stations

This space station, called Mir, was built in orbit by the Soviet Union. Astronauts worked and conducted experiments on Mir until it returned to Earth in 2001.

The crew of the ISS do not need space suits when they are inside.

The **International Space Station (ISS)** is like a research station in space. Astronauts travel to the ISS in spacecraft. Many countries send astronauts to work here. You easily can see the ISS from Earth.

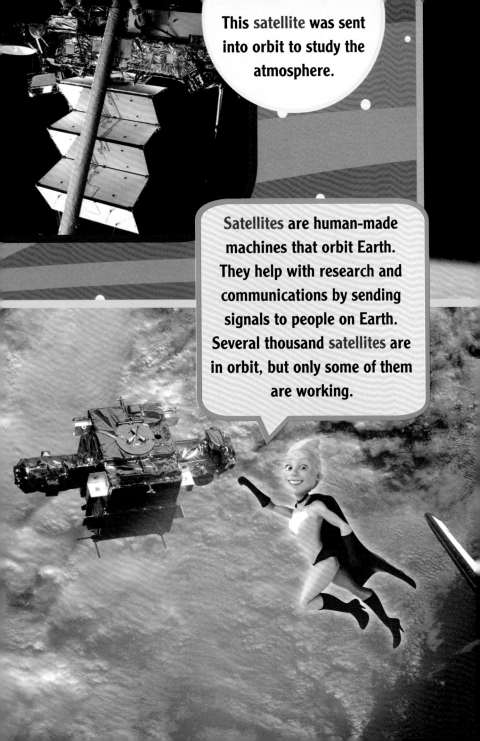

If you see a star moving slowly across the night sky, you are actually seeing a satellite reflecting sunlight as it orbits Earth.

Sometimes satellites break and need repair. Astronauts have to leave their spacecraft and "walk" in space to fix broken satellites.

Satellites

Asteroids are sometimes called minor planets. Asteroids are smaller and not as round as planets. But asteroids can have moons!

Meteoroids are similar to asteroids but they are much smaller—many are not as wide as you are tall.

Asteroids and meteoroides are made of rock and minerals, and they have unusual shapes. Like planets, asteroids orbit the Sun. There are more than a million asteroids in our solar system.

Asteroids & Meteoroids

Meteors & Meteor Showers

A **meteor shower** happens when Earth moves through a region of space with lots of asteroids and meteoroids. When they pass through the Earth's atmosphere the meteoroides burn up. The burning trail visible from Earth is called a **meteor**.

Meteor showers happen several times each year. The best meteor showers are:
- the Perseids in August
- the Orionids in October
- the Leonids in November
- the Geminids in December.

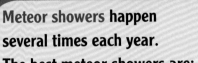

Some people call meteors shooting stars.

Craters are formed when an asteroid or meteoroid hits the surface of a planet. This crater is in Arizona, USA.

Meteorites & Craters

If a meteoroid or asteroid passes through the Earth's atmosphere and doesn't completely burn up, the remaining part of it may hit the ground. Once a meteoroid hits the ground, it is called a meteorite.

Comets

Comets are like big, dirty snowballs. They are mostly made of ice, dust and rock. The tail of the comet is made of dust and gas.

More than 5000 comets are in our solar system. Some comets pass close to Earth as they orbit the sun. Other comets pass by Earth every 20 years. Others may take hundreds or even thousands of years to return.

The main part of
the comet can be as small
as a football field or
as big as a city!

When a comet is close to Earth,
we can see it in the night sky.
Halley's Comet passes by Earth
every 75 years.

Nebulas are large clouds of dust and gases in space. Sometimes so much gas and dust collects in a nebula that stars can form inside the clouds.

Nebulas

More Beautiful Nebulas

Wings of a Butterfly Nebula

Keyhole
Nebula

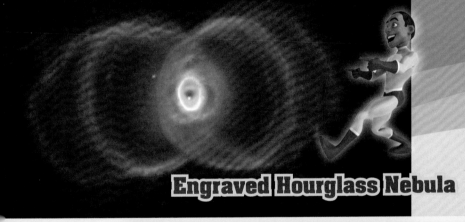

Engraved Hourglass Nebula

Calabash
Nebula

The Publisher: Super Explorers is an imprint of Blue Bike Books

Library and Archives Canada Cataloguing in Publication

Hartson, Tamara, 1974–, author
    Space / Tamara Hartson.

ISBN 978-1-926700-72-4 (softcover), 978-1-926700-73-1 (e-pub)
    1. Outer space—Juvenile literature. 2. Outer space—Exploration—Juvenile literature. I. Title.

QB500.22.H373 2017   j520   C2016-907486-2

Front cover credit: Mystic Mountain Carina Nebula, NASA.

Back cover credits: NASA/ESA

Photo Credits: All photos are courtesy of NASA/ESA except for the following: Sebastian Kaulitzki/Thinkstock 5; Comstock/Thinkstock 6; Tamara Hartson 7, 15; Romko_chuk/Thinkstock 10; Stockbyte/Thinkstock 12; ESO/VLT 26, 36; Yuriy_Kulik/Thinkstock 34; Stellarium 35abcde; Photos.com 40b; ablestock.com/Thinkstock 47; wisanuboonrawd/Thinkstock 54; Navicore 55; USGS 56; valeriopardi/Thinkstock 58.

Background Graphics: NoraVector/Thinkstock 2, 3, 7, 41; cienpies/Thinkstock 4, 5, 38, 39, 44, 45; shelma1/ Thinkstock 6, 28, 29, 40, 54; IgorZakowski/Thinkstock 8, 9, 12, 13, 18, 19, 20, 21, 32, 33, 46, 47, 48, 49, 50, 51, 56, 57, 58, 59, 62, 63; iwanara-MC/Thinkstock 16, 17, 30, 31; Yakovliev/Thinkstock 22, 23, 34, 35; Lana_Stem/Thinkstock 24, 25; DavidGrigg/Thinkstock 42, 43; macrovector/Thinkstock 55.

Superhero Illustrations: julos/Thinkstock.

Produced with the assistance of the Government of Alberta, Alberta Media Fund.

Alberta
Government

We acknowledge the financial support of the Government of Canada.

Funded by the Government of Canada
Financé par le gouvernement du Canada | Canada

PC: 28